The Burning Bush 2007

A Prophetic Vision

By: Jewel P. Gorham

PRESS

The Burning Bush 2007
by Jewel P. Gorham

Printed in the United States of America

ISBN 978-1-60266-688-7

www.xulonpress.com

CONTENTS

Dedication ix
    To the Man of God, Bishop Glen A. Staples

Chapter One: 13
    "Worship the Father in Spirit and in Truth"
    Inspired by Bishop Glen A. Staples
    Pastor of the Temple of Praise

Chapter Two: 17
    "A Prescription for Growth"

Chapter Three: 23
    "The Year of Perfection"
    Inspired by Bishop Alfred A. Owens Jr.
    Pastor of Greater Mt. Calvary Holy Church

Chapter Four: 29
    "It's Gotta Happen" – Part One
    "I'm Looking for a Miracle" – Part Two
    Inspired by Pastor Jamal Bryant
    Pastor of Empowerment Temple

Chapter Five:..39
"You Gotta Face It"
Inspired by Rev. Dr. Leon G. Lipscombe Sr.
Pastor Emeritus of Allen Chapel A.M.E. Church

Chapter Six: 43
"Don't Send Out the Invitations Yet"
Inspired by Pastor Joseph C. Robinson
Executive Director of City of Refuge Church

Chapter Seven:..47
"What About Our Children?"
Inspired by Bishop Donald Wright
Pastor of Jabbok International Fellowship

Chapter Eight: 57
"The Year of Transition"
Inspired by Pastor John K. Jenkins Sr.
Pastor of First Baptist Church of Glenarden

Chapter Nine:..65
"It Is What It Is"
Inspired by Bishop Noel Jones
Pastor of City of Refuge Church

Chapter Ten:..71
"This Time I'm Going to Win"
Inspired by Bishop Neil C. Ellis
Pastor of Mount Tabor Baptist Church

Contributors 79

Acknowledgments

I am indebted to my Master and Creator, the Lord God Almighty, for the revelation of my vision for this book. I am grateful and humbled by the blessings, love, grace, mercy and opportunity to be used by you.

I would like to extend my sincere gratitude to all the wonderful people who contributed in countless ways to assist me with completing this assignment from God.

My heartfelt appreciation to Bishop Glen A. Staples, Sr., and all the phenomenal pastors who inspired the chapters in this book. I thank God for the *rhema* words each of you spoke into my life through your messages. I appreciate all your prayers, love and support.

Additionally, I would like to acknowledge the daily encouragement I received from my review panel and prayer partners: my sister Wanda Alston, Minister Marcia Washington, Minister Michael Wingard, Minister Jason Ottley, Pastor Thomas Adebayo, Brother Anthony Williams, my aunt Mary Ann Scott and Sister Charo Robinson.

A special thank you to Mandy Duckworth, my adopted sister, who tirelessly fasted and prayed with me as we labored to perfect this project.

Thank you to my family: Grandma Pearl Cardwell, Laverne, Richard and Ebony Lee, George Gorham, Brian and Karen Owens, Ricaud and Ruth Owens, Delores Diggs, Shelia Donnelly, Ronald and Ernestine Allen, Marcellus Reid and Lakeasha Smith. Also to the Corbett family, Sister Covella Peterson, Pastor Lamar Staples, Minister Zina Pierre, Elder Billie Hall, Minister Sharon Anderson, Evangelist Ramona Moore, Deacon Christopher Dodds, Jacqui Lipscombe, the Brown family, Johnny Gaither and most importantly my daughter Maya Owens for believing in me and understanding when our family time was cut short due to the intense work schedule of this project.

Finally, thank you to everyone at Xulon Press, especially Jack Walton for his encouraging words at the start of this project. God bless.

Dedication
To the Man of God,
Bishop Glen A. Staples

At twenty years of age I had my life planned out. I was well on the road to true happiness and success with a great job, my own place, a nice car, a baby girl on the way, and Byron, "My Everything." Through this wise and loving man of God's commitment to the Lord I was drawn to follow him into a personal relationship with my Savior, Jesus Christ. Blessed to be under a greatly anointed pastor at Galilee Baptist Church, I was led to a spiritual level so deep it was beyond my complete comprehension. The Sunday I was filled with the Holy Spirit I was frightened because I didn't know what it was or what it meant. But each sermon the pastor preached offered clear resolution to whatever problems I was facing.

While I continued to grow in the Lord, Byron's desire to attend church began to fade. He knew he wasn't completely living the way God wanted him to. Whenever I inquired about his absence from church he would say, "I can't go before the Lord like this." He respected the Lord so much that even the smallest sin would bother his spirit. The presence of God was so strong in our church that Byron literally feared it would be like standing face-to-face with God on Judgment Day. In church he would have to confront his sins, but in the streets he could avoid them. His conscience hid behind his social life.

One year and one month after our daughter was born I found myself in the midst of a terrible storm. The love of my life had been shot in the head, taken away by a single bullet. When this happened, my soul died along with Byron. I struggled with thoughts of suicide, major depression and regret. I fought to praise the Lord and pushed myself to go to church, wondering why God had taken away "my everything." Not knowing how to put on the armor of God and fight the angry spirit within, I fled the church scene.

Through God's grace I ended up back in church. For the next ten years I wandered from church to church searching for the Holy Spirit I once knew. One Sunday a friend, "Sister Peterson," invited me to visit her church, the Temple of Praise. The moment I walked through the doors, the awesome presence of God wrapped loving arms around me. Week after week I hid in the back pews, thirsting for a word from this great man of God, Bishop Glen A Staples. Though I struggled with the guilt of being unfaithful to my home church, the First Baptist Church of Glenarden, my soul was renewed with the hope that there was a God and He really did love me.

I found myself falling more deeply in love with the Lord through the anointing on Bishop Staples's life. The draw to hear his next sermon was so awesome that I found myself thinking about it constantly. Losing Byron taught me that life is short and tomorrow is not promised; so as the new year approached I knew I had to decide whether to stay under the leadership of Bishop Staples or return to my home church. I prayed and asked the Lord to show me a sign. The following Sunday the bishop preached the sermon "Strategy for Your Storm." Can you believe that? The Lord spoke so clearly with just the title of that sermon, assuring me that my deliverance and destiny were at the Temple of Praise.

As I have grown spiritually and recognized the calling the Lord has on my life, I am proud to say the preaching of my spiritual father and shepherd has delivered, healed, protected and guided me through the open doors. Because of this I will operate in overflow, increase and more than enough. Words cannot express how grateful I am to be joined with this ministry, and what an honor it is for me to be able to sow seed into this fertile ground.

My decision to stay under the anointing of Bishop Staples is summed up perfectly by Proverbs 13:20: "He that walketh with wise men shall be wise: but a companion of fools shall be destroyed."

Respectfully,

Jewel Pearl Gorham

CHAPTER ONE

Worship the Father in Spirit and in Truth

John 4:24
God is a Spirit: and they that worship him must worship him in spirit and in truth.

When I think about Jesus and all He's done for me, my soul cries out, "Thank You, Jesus." After years of playing church I have grown to know God on an upfront and personal level, and I refuse to come to the house of the Lord to pretend. There are times when I have so many irrelevant issues on my mind and don't feel like being in church. Those are the days when I push myself to praise Him harder, because it took me years to understand that my breakthrough is within my praise.

I want to be clear that when I say praise I am not talking about a simple wave of the hand. I am talking about a leap, a holler, a scream and a marathon run. As Christians, we don't always like to reflect on the things we did before we were saved, but often times those are the thoughts that will take us higher into our praise. Regardless of whether or not it was ten years ago, it was once what we did, and the Lord our God hid us from being exposed. It was not because we destroyed the video tapes or burned the pictures that we were not exposed. It was through God's grace and mercy, for He sees everything we do. So many times we praise our friends because they kept our secrets and did not expose us. Well, I am here to tell you the only one we should be praising is Jesus, and the only way to do Him justice is to praise Him with all we have.

Let's reflect on how crazy we used to act when we went out to the club, consuming one drink after another, allowing ourselves to be filled with a destructive spirit. Instead of getting drunk on alcohol, we should have been getting drunk on the Word of God, allowing our souls to be filled with His Holy Spirit. We should be so high after church that we are as exhausted as we were when we left the nightclub, for we will be held accountable for our praise.

How dare any of us walk into the house of the Lord, in God's presence, and not bow down before Him. It is critical for us to focus on His presence and not His messenger. The messenger is focused. He already has a direct connection with God. So we must not focus on his tailor-made suits, alligator shoes or his thousand-dollar cuff links. We ought to draw from the message sent to us through this man of God. No matter how good that pastor looks on the pulpit, stay focused, stay focused, stay focused. Because when we don't, our God gets jealous, and we open the door for all types of destructive thoughts. Then before we know it, we have spoken against this man of God, and the curse begins. Our walk will slow. Our increase and overflow will hibernate.

Prosperity will just be a word we know how to spell and see on pictures in the dollar store.

I believe the saying "come as you are" is for the unsaved. Once you have committed your life to Christ and developed a personal relationship with God, you should come to worship Him in *spirit* and in *truth*. In *spirit* means to be of good cheer, be grateful, be clean and prayed up. In *truth* means to come with all of your faults, mistakes and sins, acknowledging that God already knows everything anyway. He is everywhere and sees everything. He is the air we breathe and the strength we receive. He is the voice of the person who said, "We all make mistakes." He is the beginning and the end. "I am Alpha and Omega, the beginning and the end, the first and the last" (Revelation 22:13).

If you find yourself having delayed reactions to the message, maybe you need to begin to prepare yourself a day before Sunday service, just as you would for a hot date. For example, ladies, you know how it goes when you think you've met Mr. Right. First you worship the material things he owns and begin feeling all good inside. Your spirits are high. Next, you start to rehearse how you are going to tell him the truth about your past. Then Saturday comes, and he has made reservations at one of the finest restaurants in town, one you've never been to before. Once the date is over, you call your girlfriends and praise him. Well, my love, what you did for Mr. Right, you must do for God on a continual basis. Allow Him to exalt your spirit. Go to Him, prepared to tell the truth, and praise Him for His understanding and forgiveness. Unlike Mr. Right who will one day throw back in your face what you told him, the Lord will wash you thoroughly from your iniquity and cleanse you from your sin. "Wash me thoroughly from mine iniquity, and cleanse me from my sin" (Psalm 51:2). What makes Him even more wonderful is that

He won't ask for anything after He has finished cleansing you. In addition, He will give you wisdom to avoid making the same mistake twice and will erase from His memory all the garbage you have laid at his feet. Praise Him, for He is worthy. Without a single match He will leave your soul on fire like a burning bush.

You must plan your day around Him. Pencil Him in to your Blackberry every day of the week and look forward to spending time in His presence. Always remember that as technology changes He remains the same. As for the "sugar mamas" who feel the need to spend eighty percent of their paycheck on Mr. Right, when we come before God He only requires ten percent. Anything else is extra and an offering of our love.

One thing about coming to Him in spirit and in truth, unlike Mr. Right, Jesus will respect you as the woman you are. He will never leave you nor forsake you, and He will give you the desires of your heart. "Let your conversation be without covetousness; and be content with such things as ye have: for he hath said, I will never leave thee, nor forsake thee" (Hebrews 13:5). If it's flowers you desire, He will plant a rose garden in your front yard. If it's a house on the water, He will build it. When you *faithfully* surrender your will to Him, He will make sure you want for nothing. He's my man of God, and I will forever worship Him in spirit and in truth.

This chapter was inspired by Bishop Glen A. Staples, Sr.
Pastor of the Temple of Praise
700 Southern Avenue, SE
Washington, DC 20032
www.thetempleofpraise.org

CHAPTER TWO

A Prescription for Growth

1 Timothy 6:11-17
But thou, O man of God, flee these things; and follow
after righteousness, godliness, faith, love, patience,
meekness.

O ften times when we feel overwhelmed, drained or even depressed our first instinct is to go out and have a good time. Maybe hooking up with some friends for a few drinks, a movie or a little retail therapy will help take our minds off whatever is dragging us down. Occasionally, circumstances become so intense that no matter what we do we just can't relieve the pressure.

Has that ever happened to you? If so, you're in good company. Many of us have experienced such storms. Just like a thunderstorm or a blizzard, no matter which way you turn, you remain exposed to its full effects unless you find shelter. I'm sure most, if not all, of you can relate since these feelings inevitably show up along life's path. No matter who you are, you are not exempt from life's passing storms. But take heart—each storm has its beginning and its end. "Beloved, think it not strange concerning the fiery trial which is to try you, as though some strange thing happened unto you: but rejoice, inasmuch as ye are partakers of Christ's sufferings; that, when his glory shall be revealed, ye may be glad also with exceeding joy" (1 Peter 4:12-13).

There is no other way. I can't make it without You, Jesus!

In 1993 I faced my toughest storm when I lost the love of my life to senseless street violence. Bryon and I met during my senior year of high school. He had everything going for him. He was an easy-going, quiet-spoken, tall, young man. His complexion was much like that of a walnut, and his humor was a bit soft and dry, which made me laugh harder at his attempts at it. Byron was loving and kind and extremely bright. He seemed interested in everything intellectual, which both fascinated and pleased me. As we grew closer, I began to adore him. We trusted each other. He became my everything, indeed my world. I sensed too that I meant much to him, and we talked about anything and everything as often as we could. We laughed uproariously, we learned from each other, and we grew closer. I soon found myself pregnant and loved it! My life seemed perfectly planned. I was well on my way to living the kind of life I wanted. Life was great, and I was filled with happiness!

Byron had just finished his second year of college where he was studying electrical engineering, made the dean's list and landed a great internship with the promise of a high-paying job upon graduation. He drove a nice car, had a great family and was blessed with good health; but rather than focusing on pursing righteousness, godliness, faith, love and meekness, he tried to play both sides of the fence, chasing after quick cash and flashy cars. As is often the case, his impatience left him with the opposite of what he desired. His parents were childless, his daughter was fatherless, and I was hopeless.

Upset with God for allowing Byron to be taken from us, I struggled to trust Him. Eventually I quit trying and left God and His church behind. Sorrow, depression, worry, anger and loneliness became my constant companions. I tried everything I could to shake them. I maxed out fourteen credit cards in retail therapy, surrounded myself with gangsters and drug dealers, hoping a stray bullet would put me out of my misery, and trusted in the uncertain riches of wealthy men. While I was trying to make myself feel better, I actually hurt myself even more.

The devil wanted me dead and did everything he could to set me up for failure. He had a strong hold on my life and took advantage of the fact that I was upset with the Lord. His strategy was to warp my way of thinking and drag me far from the truth that God really loved me, wanted to use me and would one day heal my wounded heart. At my lowest I'm sure he thought he had me, that he'd won the battle for my soul, but he underestimated the power of Love. "The thief cometh not, but for to steal, and to kill, and to destroy: I am come that they might have life, and that they might have it more abundantly" (John 10:10).

While God continued to send His angels to help and support me, I continued to push them away, determined to walk with those who were headed for self-destruction. Only through God's grace am I alive today and able to write this testimony. Praise be to my redeemer. "As far as the east is from the west, so far hath God removed our transgressions from us" (Psalm 103:12).

Slowly my life began to improve as time diminished the pain. By 1995 I had resolved my credit card problem, returned to church, opened my own business, was in a serious relationship and felt confident my daughter and I would be fine. Though the storm was subsiding, I couldn't manage to shake the depression or the habit of searching for Byron in the men I dated, so I decided to go to a psychiatrist hoping to obtain relief in the form of a prescription. I was under the assumption the doctor would write me a prescription for my pain and assure me it would make me feel better. Shortly after my appointment, with my bottle of Prozac in hand, I envisioned myself happy and healthy again. No longer would I struggle against the raging waves of grief that propelled me to the cemetery every day and robbed me of my joy, not to mention the forty pounds of flesh I had lost to it.

I'm thankful that when you are a child of God, even if you have wandered into a dangerous spot, He will send an angel to assist you in your time of need. That evening found me at home gripping my new bottle of happy pills and explaining to my boyfriend what the doctor had said. While I was talking to this older and wiser unsaved man, God showed up, took control of the situation and instructed him to snatch the bottle of pills out of my hand and dispose of them immediately. The Lord spoke boldly to my spirit saying, "My child, I have jurisdiction over your body, and the devil is defeated." As Jeremiah 1:5 says, "Before I formed thee in the belly I knew thee; and before thou camest forth out of the womb I sanctified thee, and I ordained thee a prophet unto the nations."

I sat in silence hearing the voice of Byron's and my pastor, saying, "Until you are strong enough to handle it, run; run from that which has you shackled, but pursue righteousness." As Psalm 119:32 records, "I will run the way of thy commandments, when thou shall enlarge my heart."

That familiar voice and phrase brought back memories of Byron and me sitting under this anointed man's teachings. Suddenly the memory of Byron and the tragedy of his death came flooding back, causing my tears to flow heavily again. I had been running for the past two years, but I had been running in the wrong direction. Instead of running toward righteousness I was running toward self-destruction, which landed me in the middle of a whole new set of problems. I knew the only way to come out of this storm was to face the devastation head-on. I had been avoiding it whenever anyone tried to talk about it. I had to acknowledge that it did happen and I would have to live with it. I had to allow God to have the final say and be in complete control. I needed to start to live again and trust God that He would not only bring me through the storm but He would use this sorrow to enable me to grow.

Our pastor always said to "thank God for the good and the bad. Thank Him for the little things in life." That was exactly what I should have been doing—thanking God for my baby girl who was a part of Byron. She was the apple of my eye and brought me so much joy. But instead of focusing on that joy I focused on the fact that she looked so much like her father and we would never have him with us.

Instead of creating new memories with my daughter, day after day for months on end I would visit the cemetery, looking for some sort of prescription to relieve the pounding of the storm and finally bring rest to my spirit. People couldn't understand why I needed to visit his grave so much. They told me it was unhealthy for me to dwell on this one terrible episode of my life. During my graveside vigil I forgot to recognize I had a good life. I failed to thank God for protecting me from the bullets His angels blocked from breaking my skin. The one that came through the car window and just missed my face, the one that killed Byron ten minutes after he walked away from my car and the one that lay dormant in the chamber of the gun that was held to my head. "Not that I speak in respect of want: for I have learned, in whatsoever state I am, therewith to be content" (Philippians 4:11).

Because of God's grace and mercy I live. Satan sent every sucker he had after me, but God kept me safe in the hollow of His hand. I am glad to be free and content to be saved. The God I serve will keep you. He will keep you out of the mental institution; He'll keep you from filling that prescription and overdosing. He'll keep you because He's Jesus the Christ, Jesus the Lord, Jesus the Alpha and Jesus the Omega. He's the beginning and the end, the author and the finisher of my story.

CHAPTER THREE

The Year of Perfecting

Psalm 138:8
The Lord will perfect that which concerneth me: thy
mercy, O LORD, endureth for ever: forsake not the
works of thine own hands.

Over the next few years I successfully ran my business, forged new relationships, raised my daughter with the support of her godfather and grandparents, and continued attending church. The Lord blessed me with a mature businesswoman whose mentorship helped me grow both professionally and personally. I also continued to grow closer to the Lord; but the closer I drew to Him, the more alienated I became from my worldly friends. Unfortunately, many of them started to criticize the changes God manifested in me. When God is perfecting you, there will be people who want to hold you back from your destiny. They will try to keep you right where you are by criticizing you. Some of them started treating me like an outcast because I no longer hung out with them. I felt increasingly uncomfortable around them, especially when I walked into the room and they suddenly got quiet or giggled for no apparent reason. It bothered me that they were obviously talking behind my back because I wasn't a mature Christian. I didn't handle their rejection with love, as the Bible instructs. Instead I said and did things to intentionally hurt them, which only made things worse.

By age twenty-eight my continued growth brought many changes. I sold my business, started working for someone else and stepped away from many relationships that hindered my growth. Along with those significant changes, the Lord gave me a prophetic vision concerning my future. I heard His voice speak so clearly to me saying, "You will be a millionaire by the age of thirty-five." (A prophetic vision of the future is a message given directly from God to an individual without the coming of a prophet or an evangelist to lay hands on that person.)

Since I wasn't very familiar with the Word of God or the concept of prophecy, I questioned what I heard. I didn't know I could find the answers to all my questions in the Bible. I didn't know the Scripture said, "The Lord will perfect that which concerns me." So I kept living with my faith, the size of a mustard seed, thinking over and over in my head that "if God said it, I believed it."

As my life began to unfold, I thanked God for what He had done thus far and held on to the word He gave me and the vision I created in my mind from that word. Not wanting to miss what God planned for me, I made a concentrated effort to praise Him and follow Him more closely by going to church, praying and studying the Bible. I asked Him to help me hold on to His word, no matter what life had in store for me. In all things we are to believe the promises of God and trust Him to fulfill the visions He gives us. "And, behold, I send the promise of my Father upon you: but tarry ye in the city of Jerusalem, until ye be endued with power from on high" (Luke 24:49).

God blessed every area of my life. The closer I walked with Him and allowed myself to be transformed into His image, the greater His favor became in my life. With each business venture I tackled, God continued to open doors and allowed no man to close them except me. "I know thy works: behold, I have set before thee an open door, and no man can shut it: for thou hast a little strength, and hast kept my word, and hast not denied my name" (Revelation 3:8). Because He kept me strong, my faith was untouchable. It seemed there was nothing I could not do. "Yea, though I walk through the valley of the shadow of death, I will fear no evil: for thou art with me; thy rod and thy staff they comfort me" (Psalm 23:4). Stepping out of the wilderness and into God's marvelous light I continued to hear His voice concerning my destiny. I often asked God to please let me know how I would become a millionaire. Year after year the question went unanswered, so I continued to pursue one business venture after another. When a project soured, I never felt like a failure because I stood on God's promise. I knew it was just a matter of time before one of my projects worked out for good. I understood that the blessed people in life, as well as the great men of the Bible, worked hard and never gave up. Expecting great things to happen, I kept pushing and hustling. When people would ask me what I was up to, I would often reply, "Trying to make a dollar out of fifteen cents." I was determined to increase in all areas of my life and not by the funds I withdrew from my ex-boyfriends' bank accounts. Many women would become excited if a man put her name on his account without being married. In my situation it was just a test of my faithfulness to see if I would be a good steward of their money. For me it was not important if my name was on their bank accounts. I needed my name to be written on the account of Jesus Christ; written in the Lamb's Book of Life; to see the title of lender and not borrower written under my name. I needed what God had for me, not man. I needed more than enough, the pressed-down, shaken-together, running-over increase. I needed a harvest no man could provide so my child and her children and her children's children could feast for the rest of their lives.

God's promise allowed me to see myself differently. I walked with new purpose even though His plan for me was still unclear. In my mind I created riches and glory, peace and harmony. "If God said it, I believe it."

With all the questions I asked God about His promises I never once paid attention to the fact that I would be thirty-five in the seventh year of the millennium. Seven is the number of perfection. The number of fullness, completion, full development and *maturity*. There are seven colors in the rainbow and seven days in a week, and, most important, God created the heaven and the earth and rested on the seventh day.

Being an immature Christian, I didn't catch how serious it was to receive a prophetic vision scheduled to take place in 2007. I am so grateful I serve a God who is trustworthy and true to His Word. In spite of the fact that I did not set aside intimate time with God and His Word, as I should have, He continued to bless me with His grace and mercy. I spoke about my vision being peace and harmony, riches and glory. Well, not only will I get the glory out of God's promise, He will also get the glory from how His works in me will affect the lives of those I once ran with in the streets. He will begin to brag on me to the demons I stepped over. This book will speak healing, peace, deliverance, prosperity and understanding into all of their lives, in the name of Jesus. He's my man of God. He's my "all that," and He will do it.

Now that the time has come and God has perfected my life— "If they obey and serve him, they shall spend their days in prosperity, and their years in pleasures" (Job 36:11)—I will take back what the devil stole from me, and God will set straight all the lies spoken of me. God will exalt my name above all nations and increase His favor on my life, just as He did for Joseph in Egypt. "And it came to pass from the time that he had made him overseer in his house, and over all that he had, that the Lord blessed the Egyptian's house for Joseph's sake; and the blessing of the Lord was upon all that he had in the house, and in the field" (Genesis 39:5).

I will exercise my faith and meditate within my heart as I continue to praise the name of Jesus. I will forever reflect on His goodness and all He has done for me. My spirit will rejoice and praise God, simply because He withheld nothing from me during my waiting period, even though I did not properly nourish my soul with His Word. Since I will not turn from God, I will succeed in whatever I choose to do, and light will forever shine on the road ahead of me. "Thou shalt also decree a thing, and it shall be established unto thee: and the light shall shine upon thy ways" (Job 22:28). "I am fearfully and wonderfully made" (Psalm 139:14). The anointing placed on me shines as it did on Moses' face when he spent time in God's glorious presence. Therefore I must be obedient to His will and keep His commandments. I will continue to bow down before Him for He is my master, He is my king, and He grants me the mercy to change my ways, my attitude and my ungodly desires. He cleanses my mind, my body and my soul. Yes, He is able, and if He did it for me He will do it for you. He will perfect all that concerns you, if you will allow yourself to be filled with His Spirit, to hear His voice and to walk in accordance to His will.

This chapter was inspired by Bishop Alfred A. Owens Jr.
Pastor of Greater Mt. Calvary Holy Church
Rhode Island Avenue, NW
Washington, DC
www.gmchc.org

CHAPTER FOUR

It's Gotta Happen (Part One)

John 7:21
Jesus answered and said unto them, I have done one work, and ye all marvel.

S o there I was, thirty-five years old, in the year 2006, expecting something major to happen. "It's gotta happen," I believed, simply because I was in a down place. Without a full-time job my bills were more than I could handle. I tried to make ends meet with my part-time income from the church and a few jobs from my marketing business. In addition to the usual living expenses I had a mortgage, a house being built near the water, a truck note and a credit card bill, all of which needed to be paid every month, regardless of my employment status. My elevated credit score began to decrease. The only good increase in my life that year was my tithe. During my worst financial year the Lord impressed it upon me to trust Him and increase my tithe from ten percent of my net income to fifteen percent of my gross. Regardless of the amount of my monthly expenses I vowed I would do just that, and each week that is exactly what I did and still do. So you see, the devil is a little mad, because he knows the cheerful giver will reap what they sow. In spite of the fact that I am in the toughest financial struggle of my life, I will walk by faith and not by sight. No matter what happens, my giving will not decrease. I am determined not to hold back or rob the Lord of what is His, even if He has a foreclosure planned during this time of financial hardship. In spite of my circumstances I see the big picture. I have read of the great prophets in the Bible who hit rock bottom before the Lord allowed them to see victory. Each of them along with me received a prophetic vision from the Lord. I used to run from the mountains that stood in my way; now I command them to move. "And Jesus said unto them, Because of your unbelief: for verily I say unto you, If ye have faith as a grain of mustard seed, ye shall say unto this mountain, Remove hence to yonder place; and it shall remove; and nothing shall be impossible unto you" (Matthew 17:20).

For me to be in the situation where I could not find a job had to be God's doing. I've never had a problem gaining employ-ment. In fact, God had always allowed me to gain positions for which I was not fully qualified. So as I continued to tithe and praise God, the devil got frustrated and decided to hit me where he thought it would hurt me the most. But the devil did not realize I had been made new, and the things that used to break me no longer phase me. I serve a God who is so much bigger than any situation I face.

The relationship I was in was under a major attack. God was nowhere in that relationship since my partner was Muslim and I was Christian, so we decided to end it in order to move forward. "Be ye not unequally yoked together with unbe-lievers: for what fellowship hath righteousness with unrigh-

teousness? And what communion hath light with darkness?"
(2 Corinthians 6:14).

I was still trusting God to be all that I needed. The devil went
for the knockout punch. He knew that when Byron died I was
very close to giving up, even to the point of contemplating
suicide. Though I knew the devil was on a mission to destroy
me, I was not at all prepared to find myself right back in the
same place. Earlier I spoke about several angels God sent
to help me. My dear friend Preston was a very special angel
God sent to pray for me, hold my hand during my grieving
period, rock me to sleep on those long nights when I could
not stop crying and love my baby girl when I couldn't stand
to look at her because she had the face of her father. Yeah,
the devil plays dirty, but I was in a place where no man
could have put me. My praise went higher every time I faced
another obstacle, and then came the hard hit: Preston, my
angel, my heart and a friend for life, had been killed. Taken
out by a single bullet. . .just like Byron. Sitting in the car
when he was shot. . .just like Byron. Hit in the head. . .just
like Byron. Senseless murder. . .just like Byron. As strong as
I had become, when I saw the report on the news I instantly
became weak and thought I was going to die. I needed the
Lord to heal my soul. I literally felt the knife go straight
through my heart. My baby Preston, a wonderful and kind
man of God, had been murdered, and I would never see him
again. This man whom I felt I owed my life to, the one who
saved me from facing my own death, the one who got me
back into church after I had given up, the one who loved me
with all of his heart, was gone just like that.

Preston was a true family man. He cherished his parents and
two brothers, but what saddened me most was that his two
wonderful sons would have to grow up without their precious
father. Preston always wanted children. I was so happy for

him when his sons were born, but my joy turned to sorrow when I thought of how he would not be able to attend their football games, school plays and parent-teacher conferences as he had for my daughter. I thanked God for the perfecting He had done in me since the tragedy of Byron's death. I was truly a new creation and looked at life so completely different. I began to pray and ask God to cover Preston's children and send them an angel just as He had sent Preston to me.

Because I had Jesus to comfort me and all the wonderful memories of Preston, I sat for hours talking with my best friend about the times we shared enjoying life with Preston. The more we shared, the easier it was to bear the pain. Learning from life's experiences I matured and realized that death would come and God would heal those wounded by it until they meet again. Proud of the way I handled Preston's death, I thanked God I was seasoned enough to shake the devil off and praise God through death this time around.

After three weeks of riding around with a picture of Preston and my daughter on my sun visor, a spirit of peace came over me assuring me Preston was in heaven. With that, I was able to take the picture down and store it away, knowing we would meet again.

Ready to move forward and face whatever God had in store for me, the devil wasn't through with me yet. One month and one week after Preston's death one of my closest friends, Valleo, committed suicide. Valleo was like a brother to me. We were so much alike that it was scary. On New Year's Eve he called to ask if I was going to the watch-night service at church. He knew that every December 31 I was in the house of the Lord at midnight to welcome in the new year. When I told him I was, he asked if he could join me. Spending time with him, even after we brought in the new year at church, I never once knew he was depressed and living on the edge. I fought with myself over and over because Valleo had called me several times before he took his life and I hadn't gotten a chance to call him back.

A few days before his body was found in his home, an angel dressed in a white gown with white wings came to me in the night. I couldn't see what its face looked like and was afraid because I had never seen anything like it before. I called my pastor first thing in the morning and asked him to explain what I saw. He began to thank God for allowing me to see an angel and said I was blessed because many people lived their entire lives desiring to see an angel but never did. The following night a male spirit came to me. Again I could not see his face, but he was the same size, complexion and height as Valleo. But I thought it was Preston, who had just passed away, or Byron, my daughter's father. They were all the same height, build and complexion. The next day I called my pastor again and told him what I had seen. He explained that I should not be afraid because the spirit I saw was a good spirit since it had been preceded the night before by an angel. Not understanding what I saw and why I saw it, I went to church that Sunday and cried, prayed and praised God, searching for answers to what He had exposed me to.

Three days later I walked out of Bible study and turned on my cell phone when my best friend called me screaming and crying that Valleo was dead. Taken out by a single bullet in his head, just like Byron and Preston; only this time it was self-inflicted. This explained why for three days we had not been able to contact Valleo since he had not reported to work or returned any of our calls. Rushing to the aid of his mother and his son's mother, I felt convicted for not being there for him when he called and for not praying for him or hearing his cry. When the examiners brought his body out of the house the Holy Spirit came upon me so strong that I demanded that everyone standing outside link up. I prayed like never before, declaring that Valleo's soul was gone to heaven and that his sins were washed clean. Trying to control my crying, thinking of another two children who were left behind without a father, I had no other choice but to continue praying and asking God to cover his family.

With the support of my bishop I was able to stand strong and assist the family with the funeral arrangements. While I was preparing for the funeral, the Lord clearly instructed me to use my bishop's son, who is an elder in my church, to preach the funeral and a new friend of mine, who is a minister in my church, to open in prayer. Not understanding why the Lord would instruct me to ask the elder and not the bishop, I was obedient and did exactly that. It wasn't until the day of the funeral that I found out why the Lord wanted to use the elder to preach the service. The elder started off slow and struggled with his message, but soon his story of once contemplating suicide began to unfold. As he talked about how God stepped in the very minute his life could have ended, seventy-nine people attending the home-going service came to Christ.

I'm in a place where the Lord is allowing me to see so many powerful and amazing things. As the weeks went by, I hesitated to ask Valleo's mother what he was wearing when he died, fearing she would say red sweats since that was what the spirit had on that came into my room the night after the angel visited me. I don't know why I was afraid. Probably because I had never experienced anything like this before, other than in dreams. My bishop explained to me that because the angel came the night before it symbolized that Valleo's spirit was in heaven. The bishop's wisdom on this issue comforted me and gave me the courage to ask Valleo's mother what he was wearing when he died. Certainly it was red sweats, and Valleo awaits in heaven.

Surviving the loss of two very close friends, passing the test of loneliness and walking by faith as the enemy tries to destroy me, I am expecting a miracle.

I'm Looking for a Miracle (Part Two)

For years I waited for God to tell me what I should do. I constantly asked my bishop to pray for God to tell me how He wanted to use me. He assured me God was going to do it, and my breakthrough was on the way. Not once did a jealous or envious spirit come upon me when I watched others being blessed, because I didn't want what they had; I only wanted what was mine. Finally the wait is over, and God's love for me is glorified because what God has for me is bigger than many eyes have seen. As far as the east is from the west, so great is my destiny. My coat of many colors is monogrammed with my name. There has been a shift in the heavenly places. I have angels assigned to me that travel hours ahead of me just to check out the scene and make sure no danger lies ahead of me and to move mountains that could possibly get in my way. These angels are something like the security detail the president of the United States and the mayor of the nation's capital have assigned to them; only my detail reports to Jesus that the coast is clear.

Finally, a word from God! Four days into the new year, 2007, I attended a major conference hosted by two of the area's largest churches, with one of the world's greatest speakers in town from Houston, Texas. I was so excited about being in the presence of these great preachers. I began to praise the name of Jesus for my miracle that is forthcoming. As I listened to the message delivered by the pastor, suddenly I heard the voice of God ordering me to write down the instructions for my assignment. I instantly took out a small sheet of paper and a pen, and as God dictated I wrote down the names of these great preachers. The Lord gave me the name "The Burning Bush 2007" and told me to get the message for the first Sunday sermon of this year that each of these pastors would preach. He told me I will be writing a book of reflections for my life that will be inspired by their messages, coming from as far away as Nassau in the Bahamas and as close as Baltimore, Maryland. As I continued to write down my instructions, my soul was overwhelmed with joy because eight of these pastors have played a part in my life throughout the years. Confused about where exactly the other pastor came in, I did not question God and was obedient to His request. Meditating overnight and trying to understand what exactly my assignment was, I prayed for spiritual insight.

The following day my sister threw a party at her house for my niece who was going to California to pursue her acting career. When I walked in the door my grandmother Pearl yelled my name and said, "Let me tell you what the Lord woke me up and told me about you the other night!" She then began to tell me the Lord told her I was going to make a million dollars and the million dollars would come from my writing a book that has something to do with the preachers I know. Breathless, I struggled to get out my words. I dropped to the floor at my grandmother's feet and started to cry tears of joy right in the middle of this big going-away party. I then told Pearl I had to go to my car to get a piece of paper to show her. I came back with this tiny piece of notebook paper and showed her what the Lord told me I had to do. As she began reading she started to yell out praises to the Lord. She cried as she thanked God repeatedly for His grace and mercy. We touched and agreed and prayed that God would help me complete this assignment.

As I started my new assignment I called church after church to order the first sermon of the year. I asked if they could tell me the titles so I would know more about the chapters of my book. The Lord specifically told me to write down the names of the pastors in that exact order and that the chapters had to stay in that order. As I began to receive the names of the sermons and CDs in the mail, my soul was filled with the fire of the Holy Spirit. I could feel the power of God just by reading the titles.

The titles are in direct line and order with my life story. So for once in my life I know this assignment is from God, and as long as I follow His lead I will not fail. It's gotta happen— I need a miracle!!

This chapter was inspired by Pastor Jamal Bryant
Pastor of Empowerment Temple
4217-21 Primrose Avenue
Baltimore, MD 21215
www.jamalbryant.org

CHAPTER FIVE

You Gotta Face It

Mark 14:36
And he said, Abba, Father, all things are possible
unto thee; take away this cup from me: nevertheless
not what I will, but what thou wilt.

The Enemy

Excited about my miracle and nervous at the same time, I try to reflect on the words often told to me by Rev. Lipscombe's daughter: "Be not anxious." Knowing Satan has called a state of emergency in hell because I'm so close to getting what God has for me, I consciously take baby steps. I avoid irrelevant conversations. I try to love everyone I come in contact with. I attempt to make peace with people from my past that I may have hurt along the way, simply because I don't want to deal with old news. "But I say to you, Love your enemies, bless those who curse you, do good to those who hate you, and pray for those who spitefully use you and persecute you" (Matthew 5:44). As I proceed to travel up in the elevator, I must leave those in the lobby who can't get past my mistakes. Since Satan senses I am in a place where I am dodging my enemies and resurrecting relationships, he has set someone in a position to build up an army to distract me. And I say to Satan, "If you are going to do it, do it quickly, because this elevator is moving fast and I don't have time to waste." The sad thing is that if Satan had any sense he would realize there is no demon in hell that can block this blessing by sending an immature saint to stir up old news. Misery loves company, and right now I don't have time. The bottom line is I'll keep praising and the enemy can keep planning because Jesus and I are riding this elevator to the TOP. Because He got up, I must go up!

The Sin

As I press toward the mark I fall short in sin. "I am what I am" and "I love what I love." I am a saint who's just a sinner who fell down and got back up. Just as you are under pressure when preparing to take a final exam, your mind can wander into various places. Because of the pressure your flesh will start to search for an outlet. You become weak in certain areas, and before you know it you've sinned. Needing to overcome your sin and not being able to handle it, you begin to fast, to take spiritual showers and to go into your prayer closet to repent and talk to your Daddy. "But thou, when thou prayest, enter into thy closet, and when thou hast shut thy door, pray to thy Father which is in secret: and thy Father which seeth in secret shall reward thee openly" (Matthew 6:6).

Because He lives I feel His hand of mercy, and as I approach Resurrection Sunday I am reminded that He died for my sins, and I thank Him for His shed blood. "And from Jesus Christ, who is the faithful witness, and the first begotten of the dead, and the prince of the kings of the earth. Unto him that loved us, and washed us from our sins in his own blood" (Revelation 1:5).

This chapter was inspired by the Rev. Dr. Leon G. Lipscombe
Pastor Emeritus
Allen Chapel A.M.E Church

CHAPTER SIX

Don't Send Out the Invitations Yet

Micah 7:8-9
Rejoice not against me, O mine enemy: when I fall, I shall arise; when I sit in darkness, the Lord shall be a light unto me.

I will bear the indignation of the Lord, because I have sinned against him, until he plead my cause, and execute judgment for me: he will bring me forth to the light, and I shall behold his righteousness.

As I stand strong in this tug of war between God and the devil, knowing I'm the prize and this battle is too big to be mine alone, I scream to the heavens, "Lord, this battle is not mine! It's Yours!" I proceed to ask God so many questions—for starters, "What about my wants and needs?" I have been in this place of loneliness long enough. I feel I have passed the test, and my desire now is to have a husband. As the prophetic vision begins to come to life, I desire to have a complete family so we may grow old together in riches and glory, peace and harmony.

Often times when my bishop preaches about husbands being on the way, the women in the church go crazy, praising God as never before. Every time this happens my praise is hesitant, because I want a husband, but I'm not sure that's what I need. Am I really ready to share myself with him and God? If I could only find God in this man, it just might work. If not, "Don't send out the invitations yet."

God accepts me just as I am. He doesn't care if my money is funny, if my sex life is in hibernation or if I am confused about certain things at this point in my life. If this man can't go higher with me in Christ, if he can't lie down and fast before the Lord with me and not get caught up in lust, if he doesn't have a desire to see me as I am spiritually and connect emotionally with my mind, body and soul, he's not it. "Don't send out the invitations yet."

The man I need has to appreciate God's time and operate in decency and order. He has to believe in healing so that when we are sick we can lay hands on each other and proclaim in the name of Jesus that we are healed. He needs to be able to recognize weakness so we can pray for each other's strength. We need to be the icing on each other's cake. If not, "Don't send out the invitations yet."

Will my dream of falling crazy in love manifest with this miracle? Will the man God has for me believe in me? "Lord, if marriage is what you want for me, I am ready, because You have fashioned me into the Proverbs 31 woman. I realize I am a good thing. I know who I belong to (God), and my net worth is far above rubies. If not, I'm fine with that too, because I know if You have a husband for me he will be the real thing, perfect for me in every way. You are the master matchmaker, and You are able to make it happen." I believe my marriage will not see divorce, premature death or any major disasters. I believe it will be the ride of my life, and its music will play on forever. "I am not looking for a boyfriend. I am waiting on my husband in his search for me." As Proverbs 18:22 says, "Whoso findeth a wife findeth a good thing, and obtaineth favor of the Lord."

So somebody please tell the devil not to get excited yet. In my state of loneliness I will not jump into the wrong relationship. I will wait on the Lord because I am a virtuous woman and He is my strength. I will remain confident because I have the keys. I'm locking down. I will not fall short. I will ask the Lord to help me be strong. "Rejoice not against me, O mine enemy: when I fall, I shall arise; when I sit in darkness, the Lord shall be a light unto me" (Micah 7:8).

"This little light of mine, I'm going to let it shine."

This chapter was inspired by Pastor Joseph C. Robinson
Pastor of Resurrection Church
Carson, CA
www.resurrectionchurchla.org

CHAPTER SEVEN

What About the Children?

Mark 9:17
And one of the multitude answered and said, Master,
I have brought unto thee my son, which hath a dumb
spirit.

Many times we parents are so focused on our own deliverance that we forget about leading our children to praise. It is imperative to remember that God holds us accountable for leading our children to the water. "And whosoever shall offend one of these little ones that believe in me, it is better for him that a millstone were hanged about his neck, and he were cast into the sea" (Mark 9:42).

I can't help but wonder how powerful I would be if I had known God at an early age. When I say "known God" I am talking about having a deep personal relationship with Him, praising Him, praying face down, reading the Bible, longing to have more of Him and less of me. Can you imagine God using a child such as this to minister to other schoolchildren? It gives me chills just thinking about it.

I had a great childhood, and I honor my parents for the wonderful job they did raising me. I take absolutely nothing from them. But the only time I went to church as a child was when my grandmother took me or I walked to the church on the corner with my two god-sisters. I desire to help my daughter develop a face-to-face relationship with her Creator. I long to see her so consumed with the filling of the Holy Spirit that her entire being shakes, releasing her of any ungodly spirits that may hinder her. "When Jesus saw that the people came running together, he rebuked the foul spirit, saying unto him, Thou dumb and deaf spirit, I charge thee, come out of him, and enter no more into him!" (Mark 9:25).

It is my job as her mother to equip her with the tools she needs in life. Being a single parent, I often worry about creating a solid game plan for her future. Though I've done an excellent job raising her so far, I sometimes fear failure. I thank God she has wonderful grandparents who have helped nurture this fine young lady through their impressive characters and spirit of excellence. Knowing there is no way she can make it without God, I pray, "Lord, I need You every step of the way. I need You to keep your angels encamped around my daughter as she steps onto the school bus, walks the hallways of her school and returns through the open door of our home. I am not able to be with her every moment of the day, but, Lord, You are able. So, as she faces the pressures of adolescence, allow her soul to continually connect with Yours. Hear her cry, Lord, when I am not near. Be there for her when I am frustrated. Lord, help her understand that, although the things I say may hurt, the motivation behind my words is rooted in love."

As parents, we are often too soft when it comes to disciplining our children. We allow them to make decisions on their own that we should make with God's guidance. Have you ever had a session in your home in which you and your child(ren) lay face down praising the Lord, giving thanks for the food in your refrigerator, the clothes on your backs, the provision of an education in a well-equipped school? Unlike the children in many third-world countries, our children have desks to sit in, gyms to play in, libraries to study in and cafeterias to eat in. We have to help our children identify how gracious God is. It's ok for them to see you struggle when the bills are overdue and the power has been disconnected. Don't try to hide the struggle from them by taking them to a friend's house so they won't know what's going on. No, no, no. It is good for them to sit with you in the candlelight and pray for God to supply your needs as you teach them the Scriptures relating to darkness. "But ye are a chosen generation, a royal priesthood, an holy nation, a peculiar people; that ye should shew forth the praises of him who hath called you out of darkness into his marvelous light" (1 Peter 2:9). It's the glory of the Lord that sees us through our hard times, and our children will recognize the true power of God because of it. Nights like these will create unforgettable memories for you and your child(ren) and equip them with the tools they need to conquer future struggles in order to be used by God.

If you have not been blessed with a child, the world is full of children in need of spirit-filled role models. They cry out for help because their parents are mentally ill, drug addicted, alcoholic, incarcerated or even deceased. They need someone like you to teach them how to reach God. So as we travel down life's road let us keep our eyes and ears open to the silent cries of the children around us. Pray and ask God to allow you to hear their silent cries. As He allows you to hear them, He will guide you as you lead them to living water.

Our children are our future, and it is imperative that we Christians go the extra mile to care about their salvation, their praise and their deliverance. If just a few of us will spend more time teaching our children to fight their battles with the Word of God and not with guns they find behind the dumpsters or in their parents' closets, the world would be a holier place. "Though an host should encamp against me, my heart shall not fear: though war should rise against me, in this will I be confident" (Psalm 27:3). If we would just take an interest in the music they listen to on their MP3 players and demand they download a certain percentage of praise and worship music in addition to the latest worldly hits, maybe we could light the fire of praise within them. We know they love music, and it's important for them to have this outlet. It's the music at church that takes us higher into our praise. Therefore, if you belong to a church where the praise is dead, don't keep your child from going to their best friend's church where the music is uplifting and the praise is high. "But Jesus said, Suffer the little children, and forbid them not, to come unto me: for of such is the kingdom of heaven" (Matthew 19:14). Your child should be allowed to hear the music, sing praises and dance like David. "And David danced before the Lord with all his might; and David was girded with a linen ephod" (2 Samuel 6:14). And "stand every morning to thank and praise the Lord, and likewise at evening" (1 Chronicles 23:30).

If life has hit you hard and you are worn out; if the devil has beat you to death and you show no signs or interest in the love of God or praise and worship; if you just want to be able to say that you went to church and cooked Sunday dinner the night before, then that's your prerogative. As for the kids their world is full of struggles that compound daily. Their lives are under serious attack. We have schools that are full of confused children. They think life is just about drugs, sex of all types and money. Don't just shake your head at the headlines in the newspapers. Do something! Lead them to the Lord and teach them how to praise Him. They are our future, and they need to know how to fight the enemy with the Word of God. When the temperature of life gets too hot to handle, our children need to understand that God is in control of it all. "And when all the children of Israel saw how the fire came down, and the glory of the Lord upon the house, they bowed themselves with their faces to the ground upon the pavement, and worshipped, and praised the Lord, saying, For he is good; for his mercy endureth forever" (2 Chronicles 7:3).

We live in a world where parents allow their children to walk around with skeletons on their clothes. Being a parent is more than just feeding, clothing and sheltering our children. God is responsible for that. "Therefore I say unto you, Take no thought for your life, what ye shall eat, or what ye shall drink; nor yet for your body, what ye shall put on. Is not the life more than meat, and the body than raiment?" (Matthew 6:25).

Most of us are only a paycheck or two away from being homeless so if God allows your job to end, what will you have to offer your children? Will you have a praise late in the midnight hour? Will you have a scripture to share that will give them hope? You may feel I am being too harsh, but frankly I don't care because I've had enough of people having babies just to get an extra check. We are blessed to be able to give birth and should want the best for each of our children. In order for us to raise up kings and queens, we need Jesus. He is our helper, our healer, our deliverer, our teacher, our provider and our sustainer. We have to expect that our children will grow up to be great. "Wherefore say unto the children of Israel, I am the Lord, and I will bring you out from under the burdens of the Egyptians, and I will rid you out of their bondage, and I will redeem you with a stretched out arm, and with great judgments" (Exodus 6:6).

What if God didn't care about us or our future? Where would we be? Lead your children to the living water and allow God to use them. There is no age limit when it comes to being a servant of God. As you grow in Christ, so should your children. It is up to you to make sure they know God is master, creator, beginning and end, high priest and finisher of our faith.

Why should you be in the sanctuary praising God as if you are the only one struggling and your children who deal with a variety of tough issues every day are out in the hallways of the church? Come on, people. This is not a game. Satan wants to kill our kids. "Be sober, be vigilant; because your adversary the devil, as a roaring lion, walketh about, seeking whom he may devour" (1 Peter 5:8). We need to teach our children how to suit up for the fight. "Put on the whole armour of God, that ye may be able to stand against the wiles of the devil" (Ephesians 6:11). Our kids face so many major problems that we never even know about. For example, my parents didn't know half the things you read about me in the first few chapters of this book. So the question is, does your child have a story to tell that will shock you?

Before you turn the page, pray that the Lord will help you to be a great example to His children. He will do it. He will help you see what your child's struggle is. He will build up broken family relationships. He will remove the walls that tower high between you and your children. Yes, He will do it, and your life will never be the same. Just ask Him.

Dear Children

Psalm 127:3
Lo, children are an heritage of the Lord: and the fruit
of the womb is his reward.

For those children who have been left behind, I pray the Lord will send an angel to help you grow and to be with you until the day you fly. If you are one of these kids and you are reading this book, a door has opened. I want you to know that your struggle is not for nothing. God is going to use you, and your name will be made great. You gotta face it. You gotta go through it. If you let your trust lie in God and allow Him to move in your life, you will come out on TOP. Remember to take nothing for granted and thank Him in the good and the bad, and you will have the favor of God upon your life. Put not your trust in man, only in God. Recognize that God is bigger than any problem. If you ever need Him and don't know how to connect with Him, just lift up your hands and shout, "JESUS!" He is with you. He will never leave you or forsake you. "Let your conversation be without covetousness; and be content with such things as ye have: for He hath said, I will never leave thee, nor forsake thee"

(Hebrews 13:5). You are His child, His beautiful creation and He loves you soooooo much. "Behold, what manner of love the Father hath bestowed upon us, that we should be called the sons of God: therefore the world knoweth us not, because it knew Him not" (1 John 3:1).

I beg of you to read your Bible every day and study the Scriptures, just as you would for an exam. May the joy of the Lord be your strength. "Also, thou son of man, shall it not be in the day when I take from them their strength, the joy of their glory, the desire of their eyes, and that whereupon they set their minds, their sons and their daughters" (Ezekiel 24:25). When you feel as if you can't talk to your parents or guardian, talk to God. He already knows. He's everywhere. He sees everything. He waits for your conversation.

Know that I love you and I am praying for you, JP

A final message:

As I finish the revisions on this chapter, it saddens me to sit in front of my television set and watch the reports of a massacre involving more than two dozen students on a college campus in Virginia. When I began this chapter I was struggling to decide what to write about. During the next two days the Lord kept asking, "What about the children? What about the children?" Eventually I realized He was leading me to address the need for our children to be equipped with the Word of God in order to handle difficult situations. During my time of preparation before I put pen to paper I continually heard the voice of God saying, "State of emergency. . .state of emergency." I called my pastor and asked him what he thought that meant. He replied, "I don't know, but if the Lord told you that, then I am sure He will show us." This massacre has caused a state of emergency to be called for the entire state of Virginia. Unable to move from in front of the television, I ask God, "What exactly is going on? How and why did this happen?" I can't help but wonder what the last thoughts of these children were before their lives were taken. I wonder how many of them prayed, and of those that did I wonder if they repented and asked the Lord to allow them to enter into His heavenly gates. I can't imagine being the parent of a child who attends this school during this state of emergency and not being able to connect with them by phone or the internet because of an overloaded communications system. This was my point exactly when I stated earlier that we need to make sure our children have a personal relationship with God and are equipped to handle the day-to-day pressures they may face.

In addition, it is important for us to create wonderful memories that will provide comfort in times of grief, fear and distress. With so many different signs from day to day I believe it is time for everyone to recognize that Jesus lives and will soon return. My advice to you is. . .prepare.

This chapter was inspired by Bishop Donald Wright
Pastor of Jabbok International Fellowship
2912 Ritchie Road
Forestville, MD 20747
www.jabbok.org

CHAPTER EIGHT

The Year of Transition

Joshua 1:11
Pass through the host, and command the people,
saying, Prepare you victuals; for within three days
ye shall pass over this Jordan, to go in to possess the
land, which the Lord your God giveth you to possess
it.

Thursday:

As I go through the process of being transformed from Jewel Pearl, the multitasking, hard-working, single mother, to Jewel, the multi-million-dollar author, I clearly understand why God could not have done this before now. An author is mature, serious and dedicated and a perfectionist when it comes to delivering their message. I have matured in these areas and am ready to be used by God. I am so excited about what God is doing in my life that I cannot stay focused on anything except His glory. "Lord, I want more of You. Please show me Your glory." God is so serious about my destiny that He will not allow me to get off track. He won't even allow me to date. "Yea, let none that wait on thee be ashamed: let them be ashamed which transgress without cause" (Psalm 25:3).

I thank God for Pastor Jenkins's sermon "The Year of Transition." Before Pastor Jenkins even preached the message, the Lord told me it was specifically for me. Once I got to this transitioning period, I was completely lost and did not know how to prepare for this major change. Because of God's Word I understand that each event in my life has been part of my preparation. In order to see God's glory and complete His assignment I had to go through all of the struggles and hard work. Now that I am standing flat-footed on the sidelines, ready to take off running once my miracle is handed to me, it is time for me to connect with people in this business.

For the past three days I struggled with starting chapter eight. I simply did not know what to write. On Monday I asked my prayer partners to pray for me to be able to move forward with the chapter. "For where two or three are gathered together in my name, there am I in the midst of them" (Matthew 18:20). On Tuesday I was invited to the reading and book signing of a famous author/actress. Initially this invitation was extended to one of my prayer partners. Since he was not available to attend, he asked if I would go in his place. I was excited at this opportunity to position myself in the center of these wonderful people who are already successful in the business. God is such an awesome Master. On Wednesday a trustee from a church I used to work for invited me to meet with more authors. He had no idea I was writing a book. I asked him a few questions about the event and told him I would love to go and that the Lord had used him to bless me. The awesome part about this invitation was that all the authors are

Christian women who "keep company with God." They are seven phenomenal women, full of "wisdom, abundance, life and passion." My pastor always says God will never expose you to anything you can't have, which means that once I walk into the presence of these great women I will be able to receive the same wisdom, abundance, life and passion they have. "Of fowls also of the air by sevens, the male and the female; to keep seed alive upon the face of all the earth" (Genesis 7:3). Oh, yeah, I almost forgot—they will also be serving tea. "I love tea!" God will give you even the smallest desires of your heart. "Lord, I love You!"

I am excited and also nervous about my Lord escorting me to my first real book signing three days from now (I will cross the Jordan River). "Rise ye up, take your journey, and pass over the river Arnon: behold, I have given into thine hand Sihon the Amorite, king of Heshbon, and his land: begin to possess it, and contend with him in battle" (Deuteronomy 2:24). It is going to be so awesome, especially since it is on Sunday evening, and I will be so high and full of praise from church that the favor of the God will show all over me when I enter the event.

Sunday Worship/Book Signing:

Our God is greater than life itself. Thanks to His grace, I am able to press on even though the enemy tried his best to hold me back the last few days. On the way to church I asked God to give me deliverance once I got there. When the bishop started preaching at the eight o'clock service, I sensed it was going to be one of those days in which he preached like a burning bush. Halfway through the service he called out for the Joshuas in the house and instructed every man in the building to run and leap. As I stood yelling, "Joshua, Joshua," over and over, I tried to keep myself from running with the men. I felt the Holy Spirit take over my body. For the past week I had been reading the book of Joshua since the scripture for this chapter is out of that book. The day before I found out the scripture for this chapter, my grandmother Pearl gave me a DVD of the story of Joshua. So when the bishop yelled for all the Joshuas to praise God, I thought I was going to faint. As the men in the church ran in every direction amongst the pews screaming, "Joshua! Joshua!" I literally felt the building shake. I am almost sure the people watching via web-stream could feel the Holy Spirit come into their homes. After about ten minutes of this manpower of praise, the bishop resumed preaching the message. Amazingly enough, the message was identical to the sermon Pastor Jenkins preached that inspired this chapter. The many confirmations I received over the past three months from Bishop Staples's sermons, without his even knowing about my book, are phenomenal.

At the eleven o'clock service the bishop came back out with a triple portion anointing. Ten minutes into the service people were standing on their feet and could not sit down, no matter how many times he said, "Please be seated." At the beginning of this chapter I talked about crossing the Jordan River in three days. Well, guess what the bishop preached about? He preached about crossing the Jordan River on this day. He said that this was the third day for some people in the building. I don't know if you understand what is happening, but can you feel something in your spirit? When he began to preach about what is going to happen, once we cross that river, I literally became short of breath. I took off running. I cried. I stomped. I leaped for joy, just as if no one else was in the building. When you have a genuine praise that comes from deep within your belly, God will take you to another place where you will not see anyone else besides yourself and the messenger—that is, if you even see the messenger.

When you are as high as I was on Sunday, you feel as if you can walk on water. You feel as if you can rule a nation. You feel like God's perfected child.

This was not the first time the bishop preached on what I wrote the previous week. It happens every service. When it happens, my adopted sister (who is also my ghostwriter and a new member of our Temple family) and I nudge each other and smile. Recognizing we are on the right track with the book, we are both speechless.

Sunday evening:

The book signing was a true blessing. I was able to receive words of wisdom from this author/actress. She extended a personal invitation for me to call her if I needed help completing my assignment. Just as the bishop says, "God won't expose you to anything you cannot have." Not only was I exposed to the presence of this great author, I was also exposed to a beautiful million-dollar mansion with a lake in the back.

It's Monday, and I am still meditating on the word of God that came to me in so many different forms last week. I am full of joy from church yesterday, and the devil is trying his best to steal, kill and destroy. I just got off the phone with a friend who told me an investment deal I was waiting on fell through. Not only am I in dire need of a financial break-through, but that money was also supposed to pay for the publishing of my book. I am taking the news badly. I am praying really hard, asking God why He didn't allow it to work out, knowing how much I was depending on it for so many different reasons. After I cried out to God and phoned my big sister, adopted sister and my best friend, I had to suck it up and begin to think of another plan. I needed to hear from God on how I could get the money to publish this book. I spent hours on the internet and on the phone trying to compile resources to self-publish my book with the expectation that a major publishing company will contact me once it is complete and word gets out.

I feel like maybe the Lord expects more of me than I can give. The closer I get to chapter ten, the more the enemy shows up. I feel as if I have been jumped by a gang of Satan's suckers. My emotions are out of whack. Depression and thoughts of failure are attacking me. All the plans I made to get out of this financial pit and back on track have fallen through the cracks, and I'm stressed to the max. The Lord is serious about me completing this assignment before I can receive a release. He will not allow me to do anything else but write. It is very hard to see the big picture at times because the enemy is working on me 24/7. This is the time when I have to keep my face in the Holy Bible and stay prayed up. This is when I need my prayer warriors to storm heaven with their prayers on my behalf. This is when I text my bishop with an urgent prayer request "asking him to pray for a healing for my soul." This is when I must stay away from worldly things and people who don't know Jesus. I simply cannot be distracted by man. I feel like hibernating in my house until the book is complete, which is not an option because God places people in our paths every single day that will assist in leading us to our destiny.

Even though I am weighed down and the trials of life seem too heavy to bear, I must keep moving forward. As one of my prayer warriors told me last week, "Even if I have to crawl to get what's mine. . .I will." I have always been prepared for failure, but this time it is not going down like that. I am going to march toward my destiny. So if I have to crawl, cry and call on Jesus every hour of the day, I will. I will prepare to move into my new position. I am ready to wear the new title God has waiting for me.

As I bring this chapter to a close, I would like to dedicate it to the mother of my church, Mother Louise Staples. Mother Staples was a phenomenal and highly anointed woman of God, whose major *transition* happened *seven days ago* when she went home to be with the Lord. My prayer is that for every time Mother touched my head or rubbed my back, her anointing was left behind. Rest in peace, Mother Staples; I can't wait to see you again.

This chapter was inspired by Pastor John K. Jenkins
Pastor of First Baptist Church of Glenarden
3600 Brightseat Road
Landover, MD 20785
www.fbcglenarden.org

CHAPTER NINE

It Is What It Is

Psalm 32:1
Blessed is he whose transgression is forgiven, whose
sin is covered.

Psalm 32:2
Blessed is the man unto whom the Lord imputeth not
iniquity, and in whose spirit there is no guile.

Lord, I love You with all that I am. I worship You with all of my strength, body, soul and mind. I thank You that You forgive my transgressions. I am eternally grateful that You comfort me when my guilt overpowers me.

After listening to the sermon for this chapter for the sixth time, I wrestled with what I had to be guilty for and who I needed to apologize to. I asked the Lord to reveal my faults so I could address them in this chapter. On the drive home today, May 2, I reflected on the home-going service for Mother Staples last Sunday. While doing this, I remembered

the many comments people made regarding the royal treat-
ment she received from her son right up until the moment
of her passing. Shame overwhelmed me as I recalled being
immediately convicted by those words the moment I heard
them. Standing in a room full of thousands of people, I
wondered if I was the only one guilty of this sin. I began to
think of the times I disrespected my mother with words and
hurt her feelings simply because I didn't call often enough.
I continued to hold things against her that happened over
twenty years ago. As I sit here and think about this, it brings
tears to my eyes to think that if something were to happen to
her and I never asked for her forgiveness, I could be caught
up in bondage and cursed for the rest of my life. I can't
believe it took me thirty-five years to realize why my grandmother Pearl would cry when my mother and I fought. My
grandmother Pearl would always call me, no matter who was
right or wrong, and say, "Jewel, you must honor your mother.
The Bible says, 'Honor thy father and thy mother.'" Well,
honoring my father was never hard for me because I always
placed my father on a pedestal. He was the apple of my eye
and still is. No one could tell me anything wrong about my
father. I love and honor this man so much that I would die
for him. Now you tell me, is it fair to my mother that I honor
my father and not her, the woman who gave birth to me, the
woman who struggled to keep a roof over my and my sister's
heads, clothes on our backs and food on our table? I am so
thankful the Lord has even allowed me to hear from Him,
let alone birth a book such as this, when I disobeyed one of
His ten commandments. "When you were spiritually dead
because of your sins and because you were not free from the
power of your sinful self, God made you alive with Christ,
and He forgave all of your sins" (Colossians 2:13).

I thank God for believing in me and allowing His grace
and mercy to follow me all the days of my life. I thank God

that I am a project of success in His eyes. I thank Him for the supernatural wisdom and spiritual insight He has given me. I praise His name for allowing me to let go of the past emotional wounds that I held on to for thirty-five years. I magnify His name for the thirty-four years of preparation and for allowing His promise to be more powerful than guilt. "Thou hast forgiven the iniquity of thy people, thou has covered all their sin" (Psalm 85:2). I'm grateful to the Lord that I now belong to Christ and I am a new creation. "Therefore, if any man be in Christ, he is a new creature: old things are passed away; behold, all things are become new" (2 Corinthians 5:17). He has taken my sins so far from me, as far as the east is from the west. "As far as the east is from the west, so far has He removed our transgressions from us" (Psalm 103:12). Most important, I bless His name that I am able to confess this sin before all men, and He will forgive all my sins because He always does what is right. He will cleanse me from the wrong I have done.

A part of my transition is my way of thinking and my spoken words. I can go on and on about the wrong I had done toward my mother when I was younger, but I won't because "it is what it is, I am what I am, and I did what I did." So my dear mother, Ma, I use this ink to publicly apologize to you for any disrespect I've harbored and for not honoring you as I should have. For this I ask for your forgiveness and vow that from this moment on I will honor you all the days of my life. In honor of you, my phenomenal mother, I dedicate this chapter to you for Mother's Day 2007.

My closing prayer is that this mountain of guilt will be moved in the name of Jesus and that my body will be cleansed of any toxic waste and filled completely with the spirit of forgiveness.

"Honour thy father and thy mother, as the Lord thy God hath commanded thee; that thy days may be prolonged, and that it may go well with thee, in the land which the Lord thy God giveth thee" (Deuteronomy 5:16).

This chapter was inspired by Bishop Noel Jones
Pastor of City of Refuge
14527 South San Pedro Street
Gardena, CA 90248
www.noeljonesministries.org

The Ten Commandments

Thou shalt have no other gods before me.

Thou shalt not make unto thee any graven image, or any likeness of any thing that is in heaven above, or that is in the earth beneath, or that is in the water under the earth.

Thou shalt not take the name of the Lord thy God in vain; for the Lord will not hold him guiltless that taketh His name in vain.

Remember the Sabbath day, to keep it holy.

Honour thy father and thy mother: that thy days may be long upon the land which the Lord thy God giveth thee.

Thou shalt not kill.

Thou shalt not commit adultery.

Thou shalt not steal.

Thou shalt not bear false witness against thy neighbour.

Thou shalt not covet thy neighbour's house, thou shalt not covet thy neighbour's wife, nor his manservant, nor his maidservant, nor his ox, nor his ass, nor any thing that is thy neighbour's.

CHAPTER TEN

This Time I'm Going to Win

Revelation 12:7-8
And there was war in heaven: Michael and his angels
fought against the dragon; and the dragon fought
and his angels, and prevailed not; neither was their
place found any more in heaven.

My God, my God, most gracious God of all. Lord, first I want to thank You for the rhema word that broke the curse on my life and allowed me to birth *The Burning Bush 2007.*

Today it all makes sense. All day long I've been so over-whelmed with the Holy Spirit that I have literally been shaking and short of breath. When the Lord instructed me to write Bishop Ellis's name on that small sheet of paper, I questioned, "Why not Bishop Francis from London?" Both bishops were at the Temple of Praise during our holy convo-cation in October 2006. I thought it should be Bishop Frances because the night he preached at the convocation I had an out-of-body experience. So heavy was the presence of God that evening that he preached the roof off the church, exposing all demons, commanding them to leave the building. Led by the Holy Spirit, he stepped down from the pulpit into the crowd of thousands, going from pew to pew, laying hands on the members. Suddenly he rushed through the crowd, pushing people aside as if he heard the Spirit of the Lord saying, "Move quickly; move quickly." Standing at the altar, which is where I always end up when the preaching gets good, caught up with praise, my hands stretched out to heaven, my body bent forward, my eyes full of tears, the Holy Spirit took over my body. Bishop Francis charged at me, bellowing in his deep demanding British accent, commanding, "Stretch your hands up high. You have a major assignment on your life that has been held up because of a female generational curse. I command this curse to flee and enter no more." Placing his hand on my forehead, he yelled, "Be birthed! Be birthed!" over and over; louder and louder. He would not let up off my head, saying, "I will not let up until it is birthed and the curse is broken in the name of Jesus." As he cast out the curse, my loud scream embarrassed me. I sounded like I was in labor. My eyes flooded with tears; my nose ran like a river; my body quaked, drenched in sweat. With my eyes closed and my loud scream echoing throughout the building, people praised and worshipped God for what was going on. I saw a vision of my bishop and another pastor, who was also in the building, with their hands stretched toward me, even though they were behind me. After about five minutes I collapsed to the floor. When it was over, a young lady approached me and said I was screaming as if I were in labor as Bishop Francis yelled, "Be birthed! Be birthed!" As Revelation 12:2 records, "And she being with child cried, travailing in birth, and pained to be delivered." She said the Holy Spirit moved in her at the exact same time, and when I collapsed, she collapsed. I called my bishop the next day and asked him what exactly happened. He told me, "It is all good," and that I did not need to worry.

Today, May 3, 2007, seven months later, I watched the DVD for the chapter with Bishop Ellis preaching. "It all makes sense," I realized. First, I need to tell you that when I called the Bahamas to order the sermon, the lady at the church informed me he did not preach on the first Sunday of the year. I paused when she said that; I thought, "Okay, Lord, now what?"

She said, "His last sermon was preached in 2006. But it is amazing that you would call today because he is returning to the pulpit tonight, and this message is only for the women."

My spirit ignited as I inquired, "Out of curiosity, would you happen to know what the title will be?"

She answered, "Yes, actually I do. He told everyone the title so that they will be prepared."

(Lord, I love You.)

She said the sermon was titled "This time I'm going to win!"

My tears flowed as I sat at my desk. Chapter ten, the last chapter of this book ordered by God, was titled "This time I'm going to win." I told her I wanted to order the sermon "now, not tomorrow, but now!"

She replied, "He has not even preached it yet."

And I said, "That's okay. I need it now! I called to order the CD but have been led to order the DVD. Please make sure it is in the mail to me ASAP."

She laughed and said, "I sure will."

That was during the last week in January 2007.

For the last two months I've dreamt about twins and have asked several people if they were expecting. I asked my grandmother, my prayer partners, my aunt and God what it meant. After several weeks and many inquiries it was still unclear. A week ago the Lord gave me another major assignment. I heard it as clearly as I had the assignment regarding *The Burning Bush 2007*. I grabbed a sheet of copy paper off my desk and began to write. The Lord ordered me to hold a "Young Esther Conference." Within five minutes He gave me a complete agenda. I wanted to take off running. I didn't make a connection regarding the twins until late last night while finishing chapter nine; I heard the Lord say the conference would be birthed at the same time as the book. That's when I realized I was pregnant with twins.

This morning, May 3, I woke up early. As I rushed out the door for work, I grabbed Bishop Ellis's sermon and my portable DVD player, which for some unknown reason I charged up last week. I turned on the player and began to listen to his message. He said the sermon was for a woman who was pregnant with her destiny and that she was about to give birth. My head immediately starting spinning. I began to cry as thoughts of Bishop Francis and his prophecy came to mind. I yelled out praises to the Lord and counted nine months from the convocation to the month of July, which is when the Lord told me this book will be released. "My soul says yes." I strongly encourage every woman to order a copy of this sermon.

In two months I will arrive at my full term, nine months, and ready to deliver. Hell is turning over, and the demons that attempted to make me miscarry are trembling. In July, the seventh month, the seventh year of the millennium, I will birth the twins that the Spirit of the Lord planted in me. Lord, have mercy!

As I write my final words it becomes harder because the Holy Spirit is like fire. Have you ever found anyone who could explain what it feels like to be on fire? The Holy Spirit cannot be put into words. This is why the Lord will put an anointing on this chapter to allow you to feel exactly what I am feeling at this moment. As I get closer to my due date I will breathe deep and prepare myself for the big push.

This evening:

Today I didn't have any evening meetings at work, which I was very excited about because it meant I would get home early and work on this final chapter. I e-mailed my adopted sister and ghostwriter and asked if she was up for a late night of writing. I sent a copy of the e-mail to my sister. My sister replied, "You aren't going to believe this, but the Holy Spirit told me to come to your house today and pray for you at the water where you go to pray." I was in complete agreement, as I knew I needed to pray about the meeting I scheduled the next morning to introduce this book to my bishop. I told her I would be home around six.

Once the three of us met up, we drove to the river. When we got there, my sister pulled out her Bible and said she had to read me a scripture because today would be the day

I would receive the manifestation of speaking in tongues. I must admit I was not happy about that because for thirty-five years I have never been able to speak in tongues. I've prayed to receive that gift, but it never came so I felt pressured when she said that was her purpose for coming down the road tonight. She read Acts 2:1-4 then pulled out a communion cup and wafer and instructed me to take communion before we prayed.

After I took communion she asked me where we usually stood to pray. I told her we needed to take off our shoes, and I walked her to the water's edge. The three of us joined hands as we stepped into the water in the name of the Father, the Son and the Holy Spirit. They both began to pray that I would start speaking in tongues, and as they prayed I continued to say, "Hallelujah." My sister told me to stop saying hallelujah and just let the Lord move my mouth. My adopted sister told me it had to come from my belly and to stop thinking with my head. My sister laid hands on me, and they both began to speak in tongues. I wanted to cry because I felt like it was too hard and I couldn't do it. Suddenly it happened, and I couldn't stop. I could not believe it actually happened after thirty-five years. "Now there is at Jerusalem by the sheep market a pool, which is called in the Hebrew tongue Bethesda, having five porches. In these lay a great multitude of impotent folk, of blind, halt, withered, waiting for the move of the water. For an angel went down at a certain season into the pool, and troubled the water: whosoever then first after the troubling of the water stepped in was made whole of whatsoever disease he had. And a certain man was there, which had an infirmity thirty and eight years. When Jesus saw him lie, and new that he had been now a long time in that case, he saith unto him, "Wilt thou be made whole?" (John 5:2-6). When my tongues finally concluded, I stepped out of the water and was speechless as my feet walked through the cool sand. I looked at my watch to see what time it was, and when I saw it was the seventh hour I felt the presence of the Lord near me.

We talked about the glory of the Lord the whole way home. Before sitting down to write, we shared a simple meal together, and my sister headed home. I began to share with my aunt what happened at the water. I asked her to join us as we watched Bishop Ellis's sermon. As we watched the DVD, I started writing. The Holy Spirit instructed me to anoint myself with oil before I went any further. When I came out of the bathroom, after anointing my head and both of my hands, I did not make it back to my writing pad because I began to speak in tongues and could not stop. I have absolutely never experienced anything like this in my entire life. I began to walk through the house, crying, speaking loudly in tongues and laying my hand on the bedroom doors.

I didn't understand what was happening to me, and God knew it. While I was still caught up, He instructed my adopted sister to ask me if I understood what was happening. Not being able to answer her because I could not stop speaking in tongues, I just shook my head no. She then told me I was praising the Lord with my cries and battling in the spirit with my words. She asked me, "You love the Lord so much right now, don't you?"

With tears running down my face I nodded my head yes.

She explained that when you praise God that hard it upsets the enemy, causing bondages to be broken. As I continued praising and battling, she told me my praise was also giving marching orders to row upon row of angels, sending them out all over the world to fight, break curses and bring freedom, answering the prayers that saints had been praying for years. "And the dragon was wroth with the woman, and went to make war with the remnant of her seed, which keep the commandments of God, and have the testimony of Jesus Christ" (Revelation 12:17).

Some of you reading this may be thinking, "No big deal. People speak in tongues all the time." Please believe me when I tell you this is major. For years I have desired to speak in tongues, and instead of speaking in tongues I would always hear the Lord say that the day I speak in tongues would be the day my life would be made completely new. What He told me would take place whenever I was blessed with this gift is so big.

I believe Bishop Ellis was completely correct when he said, "This time I will win." There is a celebration in my spirit. Victory is attached to my personal assignment. O taste and see that the Lord is good, and when you do, you too will win.

This chapter was inspired by Bishop Neil C. Ellis
Pastor of Mount Tabor Full Gospel Baptist Church
Willow Tree Drive & Mount Tabor Drive
P.O. Box N 9705
www.mounttabor.org

BIOGRAPHY
Bishop Glen A. Staples,
D. Min, MA
Presiding Prelate and
Senior Pastor

B ishop Glen A. Staples known around the world for his oratorical gifting and anointed ability to teach the word of God in such a profound, provocative and prophetic manner invoking the call to high praise and worship serves as presiding prelate and senior pastor of The Temple of Praise formerly known as Anna Johenning Baptist Church in the heart of South East Washington, DC. While covering more than 14,000 members and overseeing more than 35 churches in the DC metropolitan area, New York, Ohio, as well more than 200 churches in India, Nigeria and the Bahamas, Bishop Staples is lovingly known as the Pastor's Pastor.

Bishop Staples answered the call to preach in 1981, was licensed on April 14, 1982, and ordained on December 6, 1986. His love for the uplifting of Gods people led him through his journey of ministry beginning from 1982 to

1986 where he served as associate minister at Mt. Zion Baptist Church in Beckley, West Virginia. He also served as interim pastor at both Shady Grove Missionary Baptist Church and First Missionary Baptist Church also in Beckley West Virginia. From 1986 to 1990, he served as the Pastor of Shiloh Missionary Baptist Church in West Virginia. After nine years in ministry, God called Bishop Staples to relocate to the Washington, DC metropolitan area where he served as an Associate Minister at the Tenth Street Baptist Church under the spiritual guidance of Pastor A.C. Durant. One year later, he was appointed as the third Pastor of Anna Johenning Baptist Church currently known as The Temple of Praise. But, God in His infinite wisdom was not done with Dr. Staples journey, and on November 6, 2005, Bishop T.D. Jakes of the Potter's House International consecrated Dr. Staples as Bishop and Presiding Prelate.

Through his teachings more than thirty-five percent of The Temple of Praise members are now home owners with viable jobs compared to less than ten percent three years ago. In addition, through a partnership with the University of the District of Columbia - church members who render volunteer hours to after school programs with a local high school are provided with free college tuitions. Known for his strong business acumen in the area of economic development and empowerment and a proponent for quality education, healthcare, and affordable housing, Bishop Staples established the Way of the Word Community Development Corporation in an effort to better service the needs of the community. Through the CDC Bishop Staples is currently undergoing three major multi-million dollar projects in the South East community in an effort to revitalize and bring back pride to this forgotten area south of the river.

To address the dire healthcare needs of the community, he is currently developing a state of the art medical healthcare center in partnership with several local hospitals on the grounds his former edifice. Because of his desire to assist homeless women make the transition from dependency to self-sufficiency, Bishop Staples has also established an eighteen month program to house homeless women and their children providing them with life and job skills, obtain GEDs and college degrees, as well as job placements. (This facility is the largest women's transition home of its kind in the District of Columbia.) In addition, he is currently blueprinting a real estate development project to build multi-dwellings for low to moderate income and senior citizens in the community.

A native of Beckley, West Virginia, Bishop Staples holds two Bachelor of Arts degrees – Social Studies and History and Government. He also holds a Masters Degree of Education in Behavioral Disorders, a Doctorate of Ministry in Pastoral Counseling and is currently pursuing an additional Doctorate from the University of Phoenix. Bishop Staples studied in the doctoral program at Trinity Theological Seminary in Newburg, Indiana and later received an Honorary Doctorate of Divinity from the Gospel Ministry Outreach Theological Institute, Houston, Texas. Additionally, in October 2005, he was nominated to receive an Honorary Doctorate of Divinity degree from Saint Thomas Christian College, Jacksonville, Florida. Formerly a special education teacher, Bishop Staples has taught in Raleigh County West Virginia and in the Prince George's County Public School system in Maryland. He currently serves as an adjunct professor at the University of Phoenix and serves on the Board of Advisors at Nyack University.

Bishop Staples has been recognized and published in the Outstanding Men of America; the National Register of Who's

Who in Executives and Professionals, and the International Who's Who of Professionals. The American Biographical Institute Board of International Research previously nominated Bishop Staples for Man of the Year, and he was also selected one of the Outstanding Intellectuals of the 21st Century First Edition by the International Biographical Centre, Cambridge.

Bishop Staples was married to the late Martha Ann Day Staples and he is the proud father of three sons -- Glen, Elder Lamar, and Rodney; and two daughters, Jamie and Micah. He is a great Bishop, loving father, great teacher, and a Holy Ghost filled Pastor...but more important, he is truly a **SAVED MAN OF GOD!**

Join us at the TOP! The Temple of Praise - a "Life Changers Ministry" that is ever-growing with souls being saved, healed, delivered, and set free!

Bishop Alfred A. Owens Biography

Bishop Alfred A. Owens, Jr. is a native Washingtonian and a product of the D.C. Public School System. After graduating from Cardozo High School, he continued his education at Miner's D.C. Teachers College where he obtained a Bachelor of Science degree in English. In 1985, he satisfied the course requirements for a Master of Arts degree in English from Howard University, and he also received his Master of Divinity degree and Doctor of Ministry Degree from Howard University School of Divinity.

In 1966, Bishop Owens founded Christ Is The Answer Chapel which merged in 1976 with the Mt. Calvary Holy Church forming what is now known as Greater Mt. Calvary Holy Church. Bishop Owens has been blessed to see the membership grow from 7 persons in 1966 to an adult membership of nearly 7,000 persons today. Because of his faithfulness and diligence in ministry, Bishop Owens was consecrated a Bishop in the Mt. Calvary Holy Church of America, Inc. in 1988, and was appointed as the Vice Bishop in August of 2001. He has also been privileged to serve as the Dean of the Joint College of African American Pentecostal Bishops since March of 2000 and has recently been named an Adjunct Professor at Howard University School of Divinity, where he teaches classes in the field of Homiletics.

Because of Bishop Owens' sincere belief that the ministry of the church must stretch beyond the four walls of the sanctuary, Greater Mt. Calvary Holy Church has remained on the cutting edge of relevant ministry within the community. Under the pastorate of Bishop Owens, an alcohol/drug abuse program has been established, which has been named Calvary's Alternative to Alcohol and Drug Abuse (CATAADA HOUSE), the church also operates both a food and clothing bank, Calvary Christian Academy, which educates children from infants to the eighth grade, an HIV/AIDS Ministry, an employment service, a prison ministry, and several other outreach and social service ministries. The church also operates a state-of-the-art outreach facility in the inner-city called the Bishop Alfred A. Owens, Jr. Family Life Community Center.

Bishop Owens' preaching ministry has caused him to travel extensively across the United States and to such foreign territories as Africa, Canada, England, Italy, Germany, Switzerland, and the West Indies. He is the instrument the Lord used for the Mt. Calvary Holy Church to be located in California, Florida, Illinois, Texas, West Virginia, London, England; Trinidad, Jamaica, Ghana, and India. In addition to his extensive travel, Bishop Owens is also the author of "Sermons for a Victorious Life," and his latest release: "Help Thou My Unbelief".

Bishop Owens shares the pastorate of Greater Mt. Calvary Holy Church with his wife, Susie Carol Thomas Owens, to whom he has been married since 1972. Bishop Owens attributes much of his success to his wife and his sainted mother, Susie Elizabeth Crowder Owens. He and his wife have been responsible for the care and nurture of 16 foster sons and daughters who have shared in their home, and they are the natural parents of Alfred Thomas and Kristel Moneek. They also have three grandchildren: Darian, Nicholas, and William.

Pastor Jamal Bryant
Biography

R ev. Bryant is a pastor with a global mission, which is to Empower the World Through the Word. He believes that the body of Christ should be empowered in every area of life. His preaching and teaching focuses on empowering believers spiritually, developing them educationally, exposing them culturally, activating them politically and strengthening them economically.

Prior to his role as pastor, Reverend Bryant served as the director of the NAACP's youth and college division. A dynamic motivational speaker, he was responsible for over 650 youth councils and college chapters, representing over 68,000 young people in the United States, Germany and Japan. During his tenure, he held the "Stop The Violence, Start The Love Crusade", and organized the HBCU speaking tour, "Youth At Risk." His contributions have been highlighted in numerous publications, including Emerge, Sister To Sister, USA Today, and The Source. Reverend Bryant has appeared on BET, CNN, C-Span, and Politically Incorrect. He also served as a panelist on the national town hall meeting, "The State of Black America", and "The State of the Black Church", hosted by Tavis Smiley. According to Ebony Magazine, he is one of America's future leaders.

While Reverend Bryant has distinguished himself and attained great accomplishments, it is noteworthy that he failed the 11th grade and dropped out of high school. However, he later obtained a GED certificate and went on to further his education. He received a bachelor's degree in Political Science and International Studies, from Morehouse College in Atlanta, Georgia, and earned a master of divinity degree from Duke University in Durham, North Carolina. This year Reverend Bryant completed a Ph.D. in Theology at Oxford University in Great Britain.

With a mission to "Empower the World Through the Word", the "Power for Life" broadcast is heard weekly across the United States, the Caribbean, England and throughout the continent of Africa. In 2003, The Empowerment Academy, an elementary school for grades Pre-K through 2nd, and The Empowerment Temple Family Life Center opened its doors to serve the community. The church has also registered more voters than any other church in Baltimore City.

After three years of worshiping in several locations, a banquet hall, a college campus and a high school auditorium, on February 15, 2004, the Empowerment temple congregation triumphantly marched into its new 2,000 seat sanctuary located in Baltimore City. In spite of the awesome anointing on his life, Rev. Bryant is still modest enough to "keep it real." His humility allows him to connect with those from age seven to seventy.

He is the proud husband of First Lady Gizelle Bryant, and a devoted father to his precious little ladies, Topaz and

Grace. No matter how he is described, Rev. Jamal-Harrison Bryant is "Empowering the World Through the Word."

Rev., Dr. Leon G. Lipscombe, Sr. Biography

In 1948, Rev. Lipscombe accepted the call to preach the Gospel of Christ. He was licensed to preach in 1949. Rev. Lipscombe's first pastoral assignment was to pastor at Hunter Memorial AM.E. Church in Suitland, MD, which had no members. As a result of his dedicated religious work in the community, a congregation grew and became an organized church body. Under his administration, the first phase of the church's present structure was built. In 1966, Rev. Lipscombe was appointed pastor of Reid Temple A.M.E. Church in Washington, DC.

During his tenure at Reid, a number of improvements were made, among which was a new roof on the church and a new heating and air conditioning system. In 1970, Rev. Lipscombe was assigned to his present pastorate at Allen Chapel AM.E. Church, located in Southeast Washington, DC. Under his leadership at Allen, the membership has grown from 200 to 1500.

Rev. Lipscombe is an energetic, fiery, charismatic pastor who enthusiastically demonstrates his civic responsibilities.

Caring for the sick and shut-in homebound, broken-hearted and broken-spirited, rich and poor alike, he says, "preaching the Gospel of Jesus Christ reaches beyond the pulpit."

Under the pastorate of Rev.Lipscombe, additional property has been acquired, i.e., an apartment building, church parsonage, outreach building for the community, second day care center, and the Tillie Wright Home to eventually house senior citizens. In 1992, he received the Denominational Service Award for building the largest A.M.E. church within the past 50 years in the District of Columbia, consistent growth, and increased ministries to nurture congregational needs by the 2nd Episcopal District A.M.E. Church. On Sunday, April 13, 1997, through Rev. Lipscombe's expert leadership, the Allen Church family celebrated the early retirement of the mortgage on their edifice.

Rev. Lipscombe is affiliated with many community and religious groups which include: Chair, Expansion Committee of Washington Annual Conference; Chair, People's House; Trustee, Washington Annual Conference and appointed to serve on the National Presidential Prayer Breakfast Committee; Past President of the AM.E. Ministerial Alliance of Washington, DC and vicinity; Mayor's Advisory Council Member; served as Religious Liaison for the US Census for the Washington DC area and served as Secretary of the Washington Chapter of the SCLC. He is also the recipient of many awards, recognitions, and honors.

Rev. Lipscombe was married to the late Ida Rice Lipscombe, and is the father of four children:

Jacqueline, Gregory (deceased), Veldon, and Leon Jr. (deceased). He is the grandfather, great grandfather, godfather of many, and mentor to many. As an inspiring, committed and captivating spokesman for God, Rev. Lipscombe would like people in the community to see Allen Chapel as a full service ministry ministering to the whole person, 24-hours a day. He envisioned a 24-hour child care service to add to the already existing day care service, and to ease pain; create possibilities for all of God's children.

Pastor Joseph Robinson
Biography

Joseph Carlos Robinson is the Founder and Pastor of the Resurrection Church of Los Angeles, Inc. An honors graduate of Morehouse College, Pastor Robinson pursued his theological studies at Harvard Divinity School, received his Master of Business Administratrion degree from the University of Connecticut, and is presently in a doctoral-track program in Historical Theology at Fuller Theological Seminary.

Prior to founding the Resurrection Church, Pastor Robinson served the body of Christ in diverse capacities, as the Executive Pastor of City of Refuge Ministries in Gardena, California, the Executive Director of Noel Jones Ministries, and the Senior Pastor of both St. James African Methodist Episcopal Church and Allen Chapel African Methodist Episcopal Church in St. Louis, Missouri, and Hartford, Connecticut, respectively.

In addition to his extensive ministerial experiences, Pastor Robinson has a wealth of secular experiece, having worked in the Strategy Consulting and Accounting practices of international firm Cap Gemini Ernst & Young, in the Conferences and Program Development Offices of the National Urban League and its Massachussets affiliate, as a Legislative Assistant for the Honorable Congressman Floyd Flake in the 106th and 107th sessions of the United States Congress, and as an intern at the Dana–Faber Cancer Institute and the Bridge Street Community Development Corporation

Pastor Robinson has preached on three continents and 47 states, been featured in print and television media outlets, and has received numerous awards and honors, including most recently being named by the African American Pulpit Magazine as one of the "Top Ten Preachers Under 40" to watch.

A third generation preacher, Pastor Robinson is the second of three sons born to Reverend Joseph and Mrs. Lizzie Robinson, and the proud father of two sons, Malachi and Caleb.

Bishop Donald Wright Biography

B ishop Donald Anthony Wright, was born and raised in Washington, DC. He began preaching in his early 20's and assumed his first pastorate shortly thereafter. Today, Bishop Wright is the proud Pastor of Jabbok International Fellowship, a rapidly growing congregation of more than 3,000 members. Jabbok is strategically located on the outskirts of the Nation's Capitol as a church with a burden to restore the power of prayer and worship and impact the world with a clear sound of the gospel of the Kingdom

Bishop Wright serves as the Vice Presiding Bishop of the MECCA (Ministries of Excellence Challenging Christians to Advance) Fellowship, under the leadership of Bishop Andrew Turner. This fellowship consists of some 800 churches in over 20 nations.

As one who has a great compassion for the youth, In August, 2000, Bishop Wright single-handedly pioneered the first "Next Generation Youth Conference " which was held at the MCI Center in downtown, Washington, DC. This event brought together more than 15,000 young people from all over the United States to a day of nonstop prayer, praise and worship.

A central focus of Bishop Wright is that of inner healing which led to the publication of his best-seller book, "Tonight We Wrestle". He holds three doctorates in the areas of Theology, Ministry and Psychology.

Pastor John K. Jenkins
Biography

Pastor John K. Jenkins Sr. is the Senior Pastor of the First Baptist Church of Glenarden.

He is the devoted husband of Mrs. Trina Jenkins and the father of six children and grandfather of Anaya.

Coupled with the support of his wife in the ministry, Pastor Jenkins has been the Senior Pastor of this thriving metropolitan church since 1989. He was licensed to preach the Gospel of Jesus Christ in 1973, at the early age of 15. As a teenager, he was a much sought after Revivalist and Youth Minister. In February 1987, Pastor Jenkins was called to serve as the Senior Pastor of the Union Bethel Baptist Church in King George, Virginia. He faithfully served there until December 1989, when he returned to his home church, the First Baptist Church of Glenarden to become pastor. He was installed as the shepherd of First Baptist after the home going of his Pastor and Mentor, Dr. John W. Johnson.

Since his installation, the church membership has grown from 500 to more than 7,000 active members. Humility, compassion and integrity best describe the ministry of Pastor John K. Jenkins, Sr. Under his leadership, the church provides more than 104 ministries, which meet the diverse needs of the congregation and community.

On May 20, 2001, Pastor Jenkins received an honorary Doctorate of Divinity from Southern California School of Ministry in Inglewood, California.

Pastor Jenkins' ministry extends beyond the walls of the First Baptist Church of Glenarden into the metropolitan area. Pastor Jenkins serves as chairman and board member to several community organizations. He is Chairman to <u>Project Bridges</u> (a coalition of churches devoted to improving the quality of family life), Trustee for <u>Bethel University</u> and Chairman Emeritus to <u>SHABACH! Ministries, Inc.</u> (a nonprofit entity of the First Baptist Church of Glenarden). He serves on the Board of Directors for <u>Great Dads</u>, <u>Teen Challenge</u>, <u>Skinner Leadership Institute</u>, <u>Greater Prince George's Business Roundtable</u> and a local bank.

Pastor Jenkins travels extensively around the United States and throughout the world preaching and teaching the Gospel of Jesus Christ. His overseas travel includes trips to: Guyana, Ghana, Trinidad, and South Africa. His ministry has also supported work in Vietnam, West Africa, Cuba and the Ukraine.

Since 1973, Pastor Jenkins has devoted his life to winning lost souls for the Kingdom. His passion is to develop dynamic disciples who will impact the world for Jesus in such a way that families are strengthened, broken hearts are healed and those who are bound are freed.

Bishop Noel Jones
Biography

The body of Christ received a gift from God when Bishop Noel Jones was born. Therefore, it was by Divine appointment that he followed in the footsteps of his father, Bishop Robert Jones, when he acknowledged his call into ministry at the age nineteen.

Although he was raised in Jamaica under an extremely strict Pentecostal traditional system, he somehow escaped the limitations of tradition to widen his spiritual parameters to reach people of varied backgrounds and cultures. Grace Jones, along with the diversity of his other siblings probably helped a great deal. "If I could reconcile and keep peace among us, I can reconcile the Church through the power of God."

Bishop Jones' ministry uniquely promotes reconciliation and redemption, which definitely crosses denominational and social lines. His God given anointing to preach and teach from a psychological-theological platform opposed to arguing philosophical-theological church issues has strengthened and encouraged the faith of people across the globe from Seattle to Miami, from London to Africa.

His intellectual, scriptural approach, and his intense oratorical style, stimulates the intellect of people on all levels
of life. This style and approach was responsible for Tavis
Smiley flying from Washington, D.C. to Los Angeles every
weekend to attend service. Many hail his method as "being
practical, yet powerful" while penetrating the hardest of
hearts, captivating the attention of the restless and convincing
the confused that God is able to save anybody.

Bishop Jones pastors the **City of Refuge** Church in Gardena
(by Los Angeles), and upon his installment as pastor, the
membership was approximately 3,300. Some view him, as
going from "known to well known" and it is evident by the
increase of membership well over 10,000.

Bishop Jones articulates a strong statement that offers
the only real choice to the problems of the day - salvation through Jesus Christ. While reflecting on the idea that
religion seemed to offer no real relevance to the changing
climate of the times, he founded Noel Jones Ministries. The
primary focus of this ministry is to spread the gospel of Jesus
Christ through the Word via media resources.

Bishop Neil C. Ellis
Biography

After Minister Clarence and Deaconess Elva Ellis had their sixth child, due to health concerns the doctors advised them not to have any more children. So from birth, their seventh child Neil Clarence came into the world defying odds and confounding the enemy. This was to be a recurring theme in the life of one ordained from the foundation of the world as a forerunner in the Kingdom of God.

Bishop Ellis organized Mount Tabor Union Baptist Church in February of 1987 with thirteen members and since that time God has blessed this work of his faithful servant tremendously. Mount Tabor (now Full Gospel Baptist Church), is one of the fastest growing churches in The Bahamas; and over the years the Ministry has emerged as the largest and most powerful body of believers in the country. This is due in part to a membership of approximately 7,000; the dynamic, prophetic, bold, life changing messages delivered by Bishop Ellis, that are even regularly quoted in the countries House of Parliament and the profoundly practical, ground breaking style of ministry demonstrated by Mount Tabor, which has resulted in members being blessed with everything from brand new homes to educational scholarships and the provision of a group medical insurance plan.

Since its inception, Bishop Ellis has been involved in the Full Gospel Baptist Church Fellowship International and on May 3rd, 1995, he was consecrated as Bishop of Foreign Ministries. An outstanding and anointed leader, Bishop Ellis' diligence and commitment to the Fellowship has resulted in his being appointed to the newly created position of Chairman of the College of Bishops. Upon his appointment to the chair of the College of Bishops, he relinquished his position as Bishop of Foreign Ministries; however, he still serves as Regional Bishop of Full Gospel Baptist Church Fellowship – Bahamas. **Most recently, he was elevated to the position of 3rd Presiding Bishop of this International Fellowship.**

Bishop Ellis is passionate about the Word of God and its ability to transform lives. This is clearly demonstrated both in his fresh style of ministry and in the profound yet practical books that he has authored. Along with the obvious anointing of the Holy Spirit upon his life, Bishop Ellis completed the Florida extension of the New York School of Theology's Masters Degree in Pastoral Ministries program in June of 1989. He is a much sought after preacher and to date has preached throughout the Bahamas, in various Caribbean countries, in North America, Germany and Africa. NECK UP

Though continually busy and consistently seeking new ways to promote the Kingdom and elevate the Body of Christ, Bishop Ellis is very family oriented, whether it be the regular domino nights with his Ministers and Deacons or special family dinner dates with his wife and children, he determinedly carves out time to spend with both his spiritual and physical family. Bishop Ellis is married to the former Patrice

Michelle Johnson and they, along with their children, reside in West New Providence on the beautiful island of Nassau in The Bahamas.

Printed in the United States
87091LV00007B/2/A